At a Glance Series   DVD and Lesson Book

DVD Bass Fretboard Th...

T0101591

Written by Chad Johnson

Video Performers: Elton Bradman & Steven Hoffman

ISBN: 978-1-4768-0496-5

7777 W. BLUEMOUND RD. P.O. BOX 13819 MILWAUKEE, WI 53213

Visit Hal Leonard Online at
www.halleonard.com

TABLE OF CONTENTS

Introduction

Welcome to *DVD Bass Fretboard Theory*, from Hal Leonard's exciting At a Glance series. Not as in-depth and slow-paced as traditional method books, the material in *DVD Bass Fretboard Theory* is presented in a snappy and fun manner intended to have you traversing the neck in virtually no time at all. Plus, the At a Glance series uses real songs by real artists to illustrate how the concepts you're learning are applied in some of the biggest hits of all time. For example, in *DVD Bass Fretboard Theory*, you'll learn bass lines from such classics as "Money" (Pink Floyd), "Sweet Emotion" (Aerosmith), "Another One Bites the Dust" (Queen), "California Girls" (the Beach Boys), and more.

Additionally, each book in the At a Glance series comes with a DVD containing video lessons that correspond to the printed material. The DVD that accompanies this book contains four video lessons, each approximately 6 to 10 minutes in length, which correspond to each chapter. In these videos, ace instructors Elton Bradman and Steven Hoffman will show you in great detail everything from the notes on the neck to the scale shapes with which you can seriously lay down the groove. As you work through this book, try to play the examples first on your own; then check out the DVD for additional help or to see if you played them correctly. As the saying goes, "A picture is worth a thousand words." So be sure to use this invaluable tool on your quest to learning the bass fretboard.

BASS FRETBOARD LAYOUT

If you want to be truly free on the bass to move where your ear takes you, one of the first steps is learning the **layout of the fretboard**. Though it can seem daunting at first, there are many tricks and ideas we can employ to make it quite painless. In this lesson, we'll demystify that bass fretboard and shine a bright light on that wire and wood.

Though some of you may have various bits of knowledge regarding how the bass fretboard works, we're going to start from ground zero and not make any assumptions. This means we're going to start with just one string.

Each String Is a Mini-Piano That Can Only Play One Note at a Time

You can think of each string on your bass as a "mini-piano" that can only play one note at a time. Let's look at a piano keyboard for a minute.

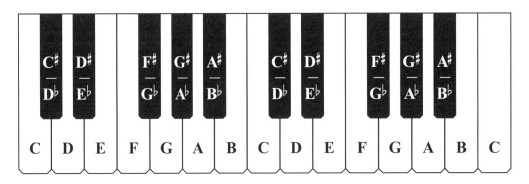

With this graphic, we can see several things:

1. The *music alphabet* consists of the letters A through G; once we reach G in the alphabet, we start over at A again.
2. There are no black keys between E and F or B and C.
3. Including the black keys, or *accidentals*, there are 12 notes before we reach an *octave*—i.e., the same note higher or lower on the keyboard.

So how does this apply to our bass? Well, let's see.

The Fourth String: E

We'll look at our E string to start with. If we begin with the open string, then every fret we progress up the neck is just like one key—black or white—on the piano keyboard.

In other words, the notes progress exactly the same up our E string as they do on a piano starting from the note E.

So the open string is E, and then the first fret is F (remember that, on the piano, there's no black key between E and F), and so on.

We can work up the entire E string this way, following the notes on the piano from E up to the octave E. It would look like this:

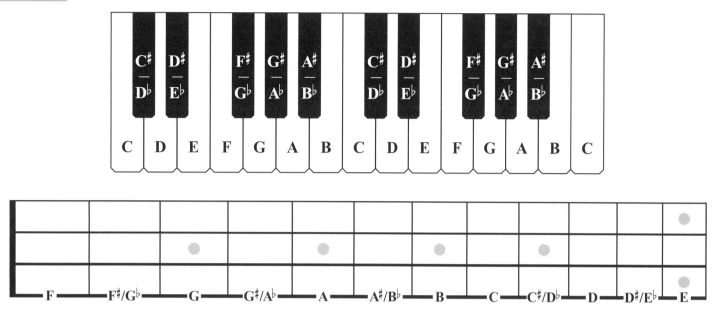

The most important thing to remember here is **one key = one fret**. In other words, each key on the piano, counting black and white, corresponds to one fret on a bass string.

BE CAREFUL WITH THE DOTS!

Though most of the natural notes—or note names that don't require an accidental—line up with the dots on the bass neck, this is not always the case. Even though G, A, and B all coincide with dots on the low E string, the ninth fret is actually C♯ or D♭. So be careful when thinking this way! It'll get you into trouble eventually.

Of course, who says you need more than the open E string to create a classic bass line? Here's Michael Anthony giving his a workout beneath Eddie's modal-mixing chord riff in Van Halen's "Runnin' with the Devil."

"RUNNIN' WITH THE DEVIL"
Van Halen

Words and Music by Edward Van Halen,
Alex Van Halen, Michael Anthony
and David Lee Roth

The Octave

Remember that we said there are twelve piano keys from one octave to the next? It's no coincidence then that, at fret 12, the note names start all over again. Fret 12 is E, fret 13 is F, fret 14 is F♯/G♭, and so on.

Check out how Richard Patrick of Filter makes use of the 12th-fret octave in this driving riff from "Hey Man Nice Shot." Patrick is in Drop D tuning here, which just means that the low E string is tuned down a whole step to D.

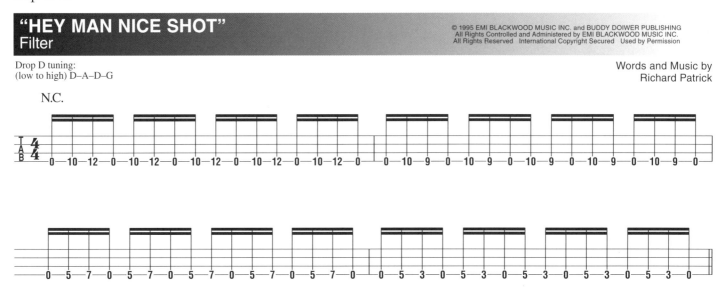

The Third String: A

Using the same procedure, we can follow the notes from A to A on the piano keyboard to learn the notes along the A string. Here's what we'll get:

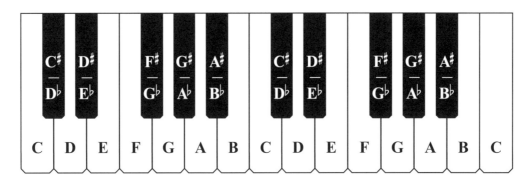

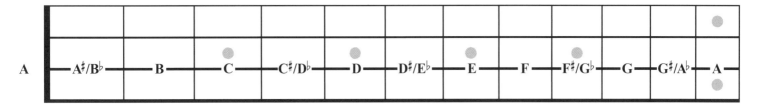

The Five-Fret Jump

Notice that, if you start on fret 5 of the E string, the notes will progress up that string in the same order that they do on the A string. Check it out on the previous diagram of the low E string (pg. 5).

This is because, again, each string is just like a piano—the progression of notes from fret to fret is exactly the same. Each one is just tuned higher than the previous one.

The Second String: D

Working up through the D string looks like this:

The First String: G

And finally, here are the notes on the G string.

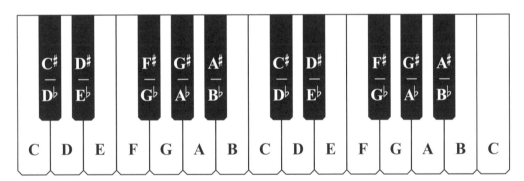

The Two Frets/Two Strings Octave Trick

Ok, so we've covered a lot of notes on a lot of frets. But really, you only need to learn half of them for now. We can use a neat trick with the E and A strings that allows us to easily learn the notes on the D and G strings.

It just so happens that, if you play a note on the E string, the same note an octave higher will appear on the D string two frets higher.

So, if we play the open E, for instance, we'll get an octave higher by playing fret 2 on the D string.

E

If we play F on fret 1 of the E string, we can also get F an octave higher by playing on fret 3 of the D string.

It works the same way with the A and G strings. If we play the open A on string 3, we'll get the A an octave higher on fret 2 of the G string.

A

And so on. This means you can use this relationship to help memorize the notes on the D and G strings. If you know that fret 7 on the E string is a B note, for example, then you can quickly find B on the D string at fret 9.

Eventually, after a while, you won't even need to use this trick, but it's sure helpful in the beginning.

In the Spencer Davis Group classic, "Gimme Some Lovin'," Muff Winwood (brother of Steve) build's the song's signature riff from nothing but an octave G shape.

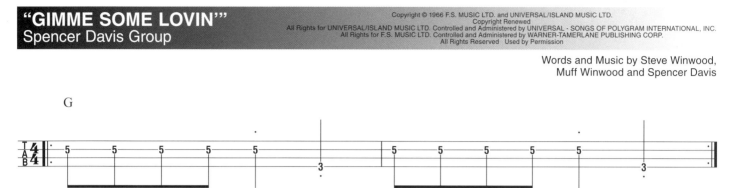

The Three Frets/Three Strings Octave Trick

There's one more octave shape trick we can use; this one applies only to the E and G strings. If you take a note on the E string, move three strings over and three frets back, then you'll end up with the same note an octave higher.

We can play a C note, for example, on fret 8 of the E string. Then, if we move three strings over to the G string and three frets back to fret 5, we end up with another C note an octave higher.

One Note All Over

Between the three/frets/three strings trick, the two frets/two strings trick, and the five-fret jump we mentioned earlier, we can easily map out one note all over the fretboard in different octaves.

Let's finish this lesson by taking a G note, for instance, and playing it in every possible location from the lowest position on the neck (not necessarily the lowest pitched) to the highest position on the neck.

The first one is the open G string.

G

 Then, we use the three frets/three strings trick to find the low G here on string 4.

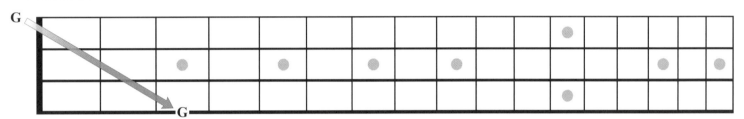

 Next, we use the two frets/two strings trick to get to this G note on string 2.

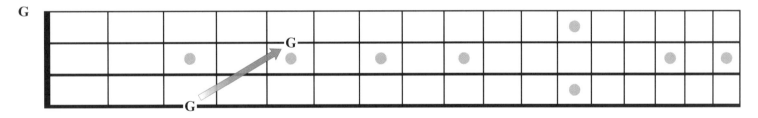

And then the five-fret jump takes us to this G at fret 10 on the A string.

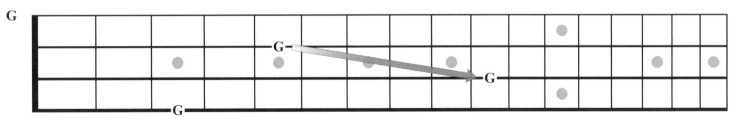

Another two-frets/two-strings trick takes us up to fret 12 of the G string.

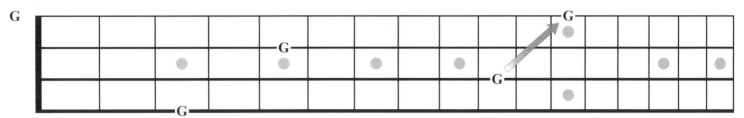

At this point, we're twelve frets up from where we started. So we can continue with the same routine: three-frets/three strings over puts us down here on the E string at fret 15.

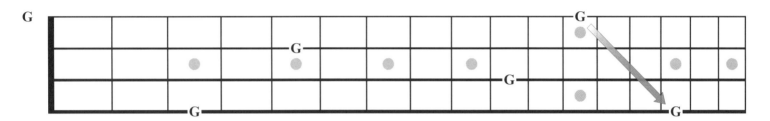

And we finish off with the two-frets/two-strings trick to reach fret 17 on the D string.

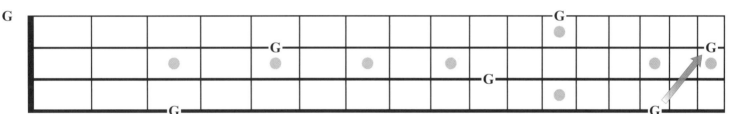

Let's see how this idea can be put to use in a bass line. In the verse of "Sweet Emotion," Aerosmith bassist Tom Hamilton riffs beneath the guitars, relying on little more than the tonic A note in several places on the neck. You can bet that he's got the A notes memorized using one of these methods.

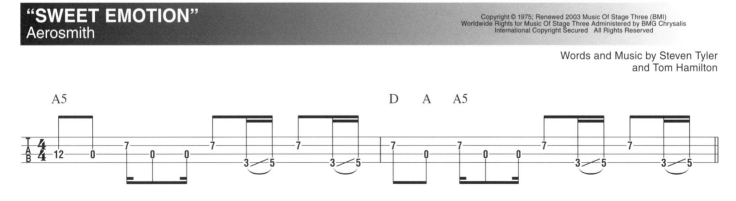

"SWEET EMOTION"
Aerosmith

Words and Music by Steven Tyler
and Tom Hamilton

You should try mapping out every instance of all twelve notes at some point. It's great practice. The more you work on this stuff, the more familiar with the fretboard you'll become. Before you know it, the neck won't seem mysterious at all. Good luck and happy exploring!

BASS INTERVAL WORKOUT

Every aspect of music—scales, chords, melodies, you name it—is comprised of intervals. If there's more than one note involved, there's an interval at play. The more you understand the concept of intervals and their sound, the more prepared you'll be to translate the music in your head to your fingers. In this lesson, we'll discuss in depth the concept of intervals and how they apply to the bass.

What Is an Interval?

So what is an interval? Well, it can basically be described as the *musical distance between two pitches*. An interval can be harmonic, in which case both notes sound together, or melodic, where the notes sound in succession. Since we usually play one note at a time on the bass, we'll deal mostly with melodic intervals in this lesson.

An interval is comprised of two parts: a *quantity* and a *quality*.

Interval Quantity

The quantity is easiest, so we'll start there. To determine an interval's quantity, all we do is count note names.

For example, if we want to know the quantity of the interval from C to E, we just count up through the alphabet.

> C is 1
> D is 2
> E is 3

So the interval quantity from C to E is a 3rd. That's all there is to the quantity.

From F to G, the interval quantity is a 2nd: F is 1, and G is 2.

Or, from E to B would be a 5th: E is 1, F is 2, G is 3, A is 4, and B is 5.

So the quantity is the easy part. Just be sure to remember that we're counting note letter names like C, D, E, etc. We're not counting frets on the bass, as in first fret, second fret, etc.

In fact, you don't even need an instrument at all to determine the quantity. You just need to know the musical alphabet (from A to G) and you need to know how to count.

Interval Quality

However, as mentioned, we also have the interval's quality to consider. This is an extra bit of information that lets us know specifically what kind of 3rd, what kind of 5th, or what kind of 6th an interval is.

For example, the interval between G to B and G to B♭ are both 3rds, but they obviously sound very different. That's where the quality comes in.

Half Steps and Whole Steps

Before we go further, we need to backtrack for just a second and talk about *half steps* and *whole steps*.

A half step is the smallest interval possible in Western music. On a bass, for example, it's the distance between one fret and the next on one string. Refer back to the earlier "mini-piano" lesson for more detail.

This is a half step:

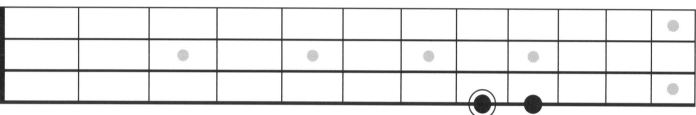

A whole step, as you may have guessed, is the distance of two half steps. So, it's the distance of two frets on the same string.

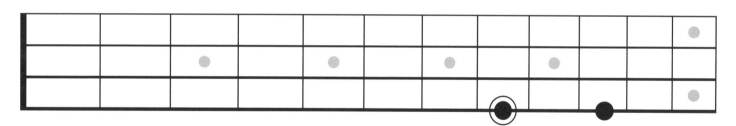

Sometimes you need nothing more than a whole step to build a bass line for a whole section of a song, as is demonstrated here with Michael Anthony's riff in Van Halen's cover of the Kinks' "You Really Got Me."

Words and Music by
Ray Davies

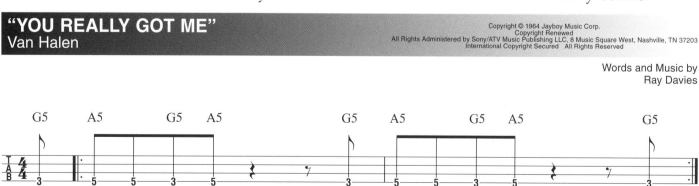

"YOU REALLY GOT ME"
Van Halen

We use these two terms when measuring the quality of other intervals. To understand these, let's look at a chart that measures the interval of each of the twelve notes against a low C root note.

Notes	Number of Half Steps	Name of Interval (quality and quantity)	Abbreviation
C to C	0	perfect unison	P1
C to D♭	1	minor 2nd	m2
C to D	2	major 2nd	M2
C to E♭	3	minor 3rd	m3
C to E	4	major 3rd	M3
C to F	5	perfect 4th	P4
C to G♭	6	diminished 5th	d5
C to G	7	perfect 5th	P5
C to A♭	8	minor 6th	m6
C to A	9	major 6th	M6
C to B♭	10	minor 7th	m7
C to B	11	major 7th	M7
C to C	12	perfect octave	P8

It'll take a while for all this to sink in, but let's check out a few truths we can deduce from this table.

1. The qualities of major and minor apply to 2nds, 3rds, 6ths, and 7ths.
2. The quality of perfect applies to unisons, 4ths, 5ths, and octaves.
3. A minor interval is one half step smaller than its companion major interval. In other words, from C to D is a major 2nd, but from C to D♭ is a minor 2nd.
4. A diminished interval is one half step smaller than its companion perfect interval. In other words, from C to G is a perfect 5th, but from C to G♭ is a diminished 5th.

Realize that we have another name for two of these intervals. A whole step is the same thing as a major 2nd, whereas a half step is the same thing as a minor 2nd.

Now let's look at the chart again using the *enharmonic* names for the accidental notes. In other words, we'll use the sharp names instead of the flat names.

Notes	Number of Half Steps	Name of Interval (quality and quantity)	Abbreviation
C to C	0	perfect unison	P1
C to C♯	1	augmented unison	A1
C to D	2	major 2nd	M2
C to D♯	3	augmented 2nd	A2
C to E	4	major 3rd	M3
C to F	5	perfect 4th	P4
C to F♯	6	augmented 4th	A4
C to G	7	perfect 5th	P5
C to G♯	8	augmented 5th	A5
C to A	9	major 6th	M6
C to A♯	10	augmented 6th	A6
C to B	11	major 7th	M7
C to C	12	perfect octave	P8

This looks pretty crazy, huh? All of the sudden, we see all these augmented intervals. From this chart, we can add to our deductions from the previous one:

1. There are two different names for many intervals, depending upon which enharmonic name you use for a note.

2. An augmented interval is one half step larger than its companion perfect or major interval. In other words, from C to D is a major 2nd, but from C to D# is an augmented 2nd. From C to F is a perfect 4th, but from C to F# is an augmented 4th.

Same Sound, Different Name

Now, if you look at the two charts, you'll see that the distance of three half steps, for example, can either be called a minor 3rd or an augmented 2nd. How do we know which one it is? There's no way to tell by listening to it; they sound the same.

But if you have a musical context, you always refer to the **quantity** of the interval when determining the name.

From C to D# is called an **augmented 2nd** because only **two** note names are involved: C and D.

From C to E♭ is called a **minor 3rd** because **three** note names are involved: C, D, and E.

So even though an interval might sound the same, they can have different names depending on the musical situation.

Playing the Shapes

So that's enough talk. Let's start playing these things. We'll play them all from the note C, but be aware that these interval shapes will remain the same when played from any root note. Also, we're interested here in commonly used shapes, so we'll stay in position within a range of a few frets above or below the root note C, rather than traveling way up the neck on the same string.

Minor 2nd

Here's a minor 2nd, from C to D♭:

This interval was of course famously exploited by John Williams in the *Jaws* theme.

Major 2nd

Next we have a major 2nd, from C to D. This is played commonly in two ways. It can be on the same string…

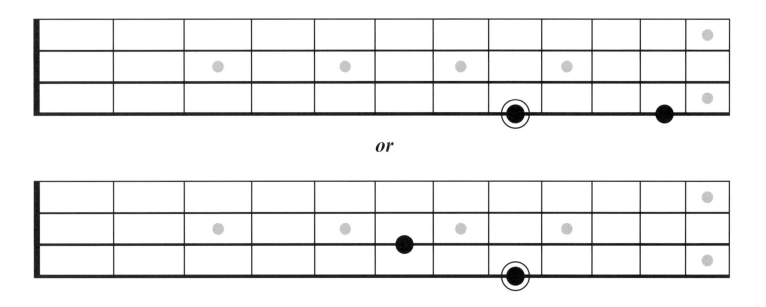

…or on adjacent strings. Doing it this way requires a little bit of a stretch.

Minor 3rd

Next up is the minor 3rd, from C to E♭. We'll play this one in two ways as well—on the same string and on the adjacent string.

or

James Jamerson's bass line from Marvin Gaye's "I Heard It Through the Grapevine" is built upon a minor 3rd interval from E♭ to G♭. Here the minor 3rds are played on adjacent strings.

"I HEARD IT THROUGH THE GRAPEVINE"
Marvin Gaye

Words and Music by Norman J. Whitfield
and Barrett Strong

Major 3rd

And here's a major 3rd, from C to E. Although we could play a major 3rd interval on the same string, that's going to require a big stretch. So we'll just play the notes on adjacent strings.

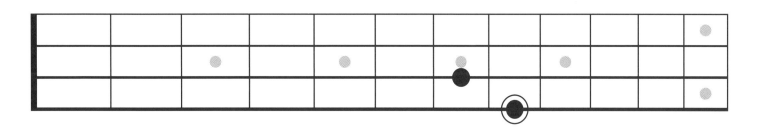

Perfect 4th

Next is the perfect 4th, from C to F:

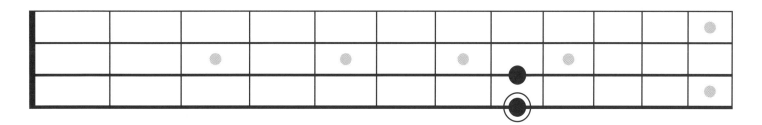

This is, of course, the first interval from "Here Comes the Bride."

A very common use of the 4th interval occurs between the root of a chord and its 5th degree, which lies the interval of a 4th below. This is demonstrated with the classic line in Queen and David Bowie's "Under Pressure," which was of course later infamously sampled by Vanilla Ice for "Ice Ice Baby."

"UNDER PRESSURE"
Queen and David Bowie

Words and Music by Freddie Mercury, John Deacon,
Brian May, Roger Taylor and David Bowie

Augmented 4th

This brings us to the augmented 4th, from C to F♯:

This interval is also known as a *tritone* because it's the distance of three whole steps from the root. It divides the octave in half and sounds quite menacing. Because of its ominous quality, you'll hear this interval used often in metal.

Perfect 5th

Then we have the perfect 5th, from C to G:

When you play these notes as a dyad, you have what's known as a power chord, which is the most common chord on guitar in rock and metal music.

On bass, we alternate the root with the 5th sometimes to create some interest and movement. Jamerson's famous bass intro on the Temptations' "My Girl" consisted of going back and forth between nothing more than a perfect 5th interval: G down to C.

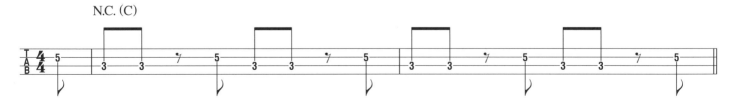

"MY GIRL"
The Temptations

Words and Music by William "Smokey" Robinson
and Ronald White

Mimicking Kurt Cobain's clever guitar riff, Nirvana bassist Krist Novoselic alternates between two intervals in the main riff of "Come as You Are": a minor 3rd (F♯ to A) and a perfect 5th (E to B).

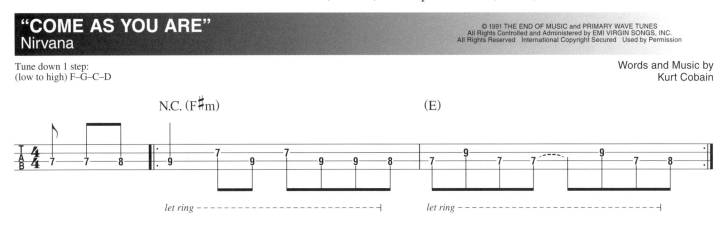

Minor 6th

Next we have the minor 6th, from C to A♭. We'll look at two ways to play this one:

On adjacent strings…

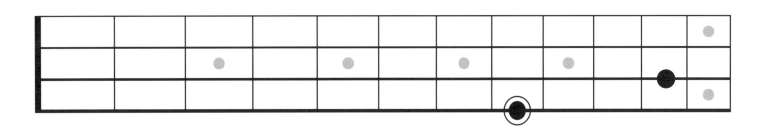

And non-adjacent strings.

Major 6th

Moving up one more half step gives us the major 6th, from C to A. You may recognize this interval as the first two notes of the NBC theme.

Check out how the intro from "California Girls" features many of these intervals in tandem: major 6th (B up to G#), perfect 5th (B up to F#), perfect 4th (B up to F#), major 3rd (D# down to B), and major 2nd (B up to C#).

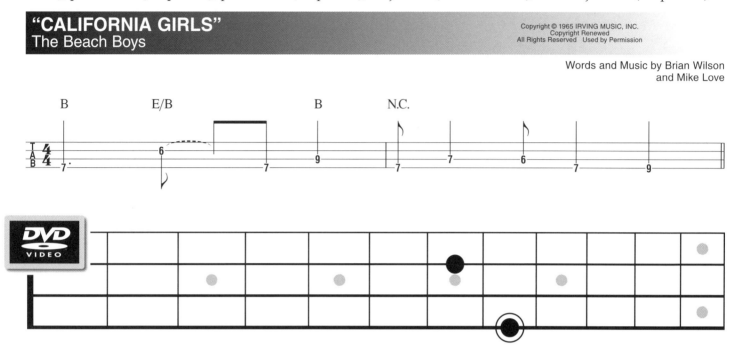

"CALIFORNIA GIRLS"
The Beach Boys

Words and Music by Brian Wilson
and Mike Love

Minor 7th

Next up is the minor 7th, from C to B♭. The minor 7th is the famous first interval of the *Star Trek* theme. It's easy to visualize because it's played on the same fret, just two strings away.

Major 7th

After that, we have the major 7th, from C to B:

You can really feel this one want to resolve to…

Octave

The octave, from C to C:

An octave interval opens the famous song "Somewhere Over the Rainbow."

So that's it. We've covered every possible interval within the scope of a full octave. Of course, as we mentioned earlier, many of these have other enharmonic names, but we looked at their most commonly used names. The only exception is the tritone; we presented the shape as the augmented 4th, but it's just as commonly seen as a diminished 5th as well.

Ear Training

Now, you have two ear-training homework assignments:

1. Record yourself playing various intervals at random. For example, play a major 3rd from C, then a minor 6th, then a major 7th, etc. Record a bunch of them like that and leave a bit of space between each one. Then, listen back to it and see if you can identify the intervals by ear.

You can start off playing them all from the same root. Once you can identify all those correctly, then try playing them from different roots. Every interval has a very specific sound, so once you've become familiar with its sound, even if you start on a different root, you should still be able to discern the interval by ear.

2. When you're able to identify all the intervals in the first exercise, try writing out a bunch of random intervals in a row. Then play a root note—C, for instance—and finally, try to sing the interval.

So if we had a major 3rd, for example, you'd play the C root note and then sing a major 3rd above that, which would be an E note. Then, check yourself by playing the pitch on the bass.

If you do this regularly, your ear will improve by leaps and bounds, and you'll soon be able to play things you hear on recordings—or things you hear in your head—quickly and without fumbling around for the right pitches.

Well that wraps up our interval workout. To continue your studies, check out compound intervals, which span past the octave. Good luck!

SCALE CONSTRUCTION

Learning and playing scale shapes on the bass is good practice for your fingers, but unless you know what's going on with the notes—and why they're arranged the way they are—you're missing out on a big part of the picture. In this lesson, we'll learn all about the construction of the major and minor scales.

Whole Steps and Half Steps

The story of scale construction begins with two intervals: the **whole step** and the **half step**. We talked about these very important building blocks in the earlier lessons, now let's quickly review them and see how they're used as the foundation for building scales.

 On the bass, these are quite easy to visualize and play. A half step is the smallest interval we have in Western music; it's the distance of one fret on a bass string. For example, from fret 2 on the D string to fret 3 is a half step.

 A whole step, as you may have guessed, is twice that of a half step—or two frets. So, from fret 2 on the D string to fret 4 is a whole step.

With these two intervals, we have the building blocks we need to construct almost any scale we want.

The Major Scale

Every scale is built from a certain *intervallic formula*—or a certain arrangement of whole and half steps. We'll start with the major scale, which is by far the most widely used scale in all of Western music. There are seven different notes in a major scale, with the "eighth" note simply being the same as the first, but an octave higher:

Major Scale Formula
Every major scale, regardless of the root, follows the same major scale formula:

Whole step, Whole step, Half step, Whole step, Whole step, Whole step, Half step

Let's build a C major scale on one string to see how this works.

Starting at C on fret 3 of the A string, we simply follow the formula, moving two frets for whole steps and one fret for half steps.

C Major Scale on One String

C
Whole step to D
Whole step to E
Half step to F
Whole step to G
Whole step to A
Whole step to B
Half step back up to C

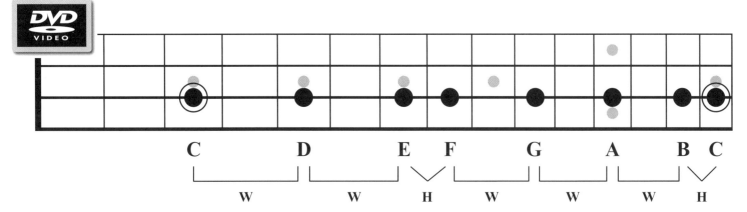

That's it. If you noticed, this scale contains only natural notes—no accidentals. This is the only major scale that can make such a claim.

If you look at these notes on a piano keyboard, you'll see that they're all white keys. Any other major scale will require at least one sharp or flat (a black key).

To test this, let's build an A major scale on the same string and see what we get.

We'll start with the open A string and again follow the same major scale formula.

A Major Scale on One String

A
Whole step to B
Whole step to C♯
Half step to D
Whole step to E
Whole step to F♯
Whole step to G♯
Half step back up to A

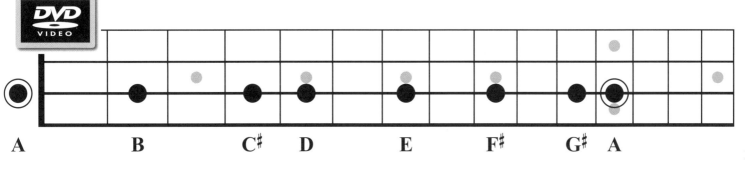

Notice that, in an A major scale, we have three sharp notes: C♯, F♯, and G♯. This happens because we have to adhere to our formula. From A to B is a whole step, but from B to C is only a half step. The formula says we need a whole step there. So we have to raise C a half step to C♯. The same thing happens again with our F and G notes. We need to adjust them so we can stick to the formula, and the result is that we get F♯ and G♯ instead in this scale.

This is why each of the 12 major scales contains different notes.

ENHARMONIC NOTES

Now, you may have wondered why we used C♯ instead of D♭, or why we used F♯ instead of G♭. The term for two notes that sound the same but are spelled differently is enharmonic. C♯, for example, is enharmonic to D♭.

In a major scale, we need to have *all seven alphabetic note names* accounted for. So, since we already have a D in the A major scale at fret 5, we can't call the note on fret 4 a D♭—the letter D is already accounted for. So we call it a C♯.

Because of this, a major scale will either contain sharp notes or flat notes—but never both. If you're trying to spell a major scale and end up with a flat note and a sharp note in the same scale, that's a good indication that you've made a mistake somewhere in the process.

To avoid this problem, simply start by writing out the notes of the alphabet from one to the octave. To spell an A major scale, for example, first write out the letters from A to A.

A   B   C   D   E   F   G   A

Then work through the formula, making adjustments as necessary by raising or lowering the notes.

A   B   C♯   D   E   F♯   G♯   A

If you follow this method, you should always end up with the correct spelling.

Since A major contains sharps in its major scale, we call it a sharp key.

Though it's not common to play entire scales on one string, it is possible to groove on a portion of the scale, especially when the song is in a key that matches one of the open strings of the bass. Check out Colin Greenwood's line that fuels Radiohead's "National Anthem." Based off the open D string, he uses notes from the D major scale (F♯ and E) as well as including one chromatic note (F), which is found in the D minor scale.

"NATIONAL ANTHEM"
Radiohead

Words and Music by Thomas Yorke,
Jonathan Greenwood, Colin Greenwood,
Edward O'Brien and Philip Selway

N.C.

Let's try building one more major scale: F major. We'll start with the low F on the fourth string.

F Major Scale on One String

F
Whole step to G
Whole step to A
Now we need a half step, so we need to make the B note a B♭
Then a whole step to C
Whole step to D
Whole step to E
Half step back up to F

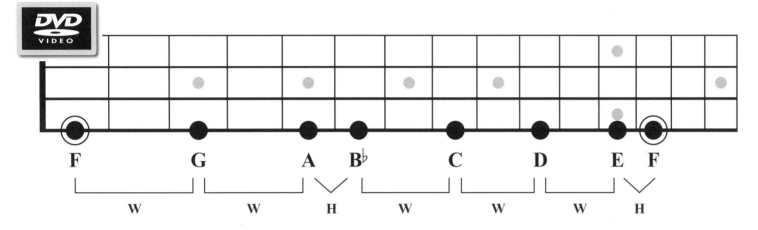

So the F major scale needed one flat: B♭. Therefore, we say that F major is one of the flat keys.

Organization of Keys

Let's look at how the keys are organized in terms of sharps and flats.

C major contains no sharps or flats.
The sharp keys are G, D, A, E, and B.
The flat keys are F, B♭, E♭, A♭, and D♭.

That's 11 keys there. The last one is a bit tricky and will appear either as F♯, which contains six sharps, or G♭, which contains six flats. It's pretty hairy either way.

Major Scale Pattern

Of course, we don't normally play scales along only one string. We just did that here to make it easier to track the whole and half steps. To create our familiar C major scale pattern across several strings, we transfer the notes to higher strings so we can stay in one position.

If we begin with our second finger on C at fret 3, string 3, we can arrange the tones to fall neatly into second position.

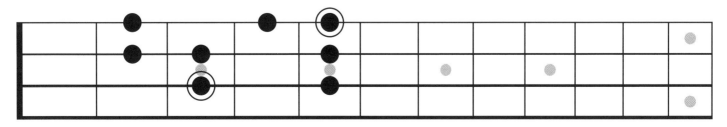

The Minor Scale

Ok, now it's time to examine the minor scale. But before we do that, we're going to take a quick detour and look at another kind of scale formula. We already learned that a major scale adheres to the *intervallic formula* of whole, whole, half, whole, whole, whole, half.

But we can also define a scale by its *numeric formula*. This involves giving each note a number and adjusting them as necessary with a sharp or flat.

 The major scale is the standard by which we measure all other scales. So we say that its numeric formula is simply 1–2–3–4–5–6–7. (When you reach the high C note, you can either call it 8 or 1.)

Why do we do this? Well, it makes spelling other scales really easy. Instead of learning different patterns of whole and half steps for every scale, we just simply alter these numbers to create the new scale.

 The numeric formula for the minor scale, for example, is 1–2–♭3–4–5–♭6–♭7. This means that, to change our C major scale to a C minor scale, we just need to lower the 3rd, 6th, and 7th notes by a half step. In this fingering below, we are playing the ♭3th and ♭6th notes on the lower-pitched adjacent strings rather than on the same string, to avoid a stretch-y fingering that might be hard to play.

So we'll end up with:

C–D–E♭–F–G–A♭–B♭–C

 Of course, the minor scale does have an intervallic formula as well, which is:

Whole step, Half step, Whole step, Whole step, Half step, Whole step, Whole step

Let's confirm this with a C minor scale on one string. We start with C on fret 3 of string 3 again.

C Minor Scale on One String

C
Whole step to D
Half step to E♭
Whole step to F
Whole step to G
Half step to A♭
Whole step to B♭
Whole step up to C

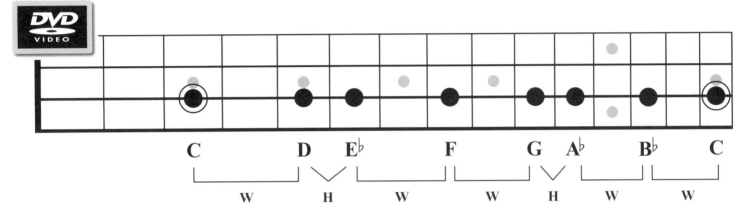

The bass line in Heart's "Barracuda" begins with just the first few notes from the E minor scale and is anchored on the open E string.

"BARRACUDA"
Heart

Words and Music by Nancy Wilson,
Ann Wilson, Michael Derosier
and Roger Fisher

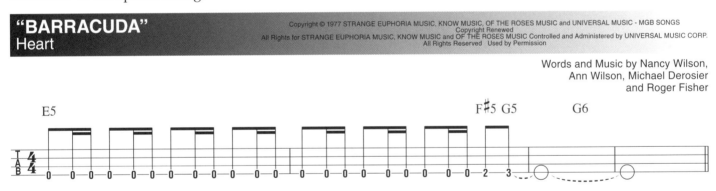

Similarly, Queen's "Another One Bites the Dust" is also in E minor (though the recording sounds a 1/4 step sharp), and John Deacon "bases" his line off the open E as well.

"ANOTHER ONE BITES THE DUST"
Queen

Words and Music by
John Deacon

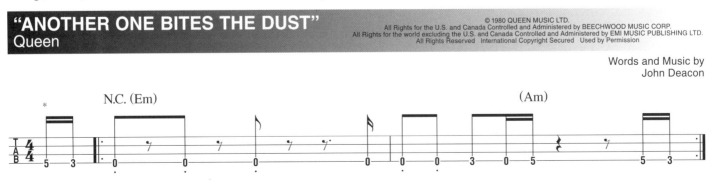

*Recording sounds 1/2 step higher.

Minor Scale Pattern

When we transfer those notes to higher strings, of course, we end up with the familiar C minor scale pattern in third position.

Again, the numeric formula is a quick, convenient method for spelling scales, so I definitely recommend becoming familiar with that method.

The key things to remember are that a major or minor scale has to have all seven alphabetic note names accounted for and they must follow their respective formulas. If you remember those two things, you'll be able to spell any major or minor scale easily. Good luck!

SCALE SHAPES AND GROOVE BOXES FOR THE BASS

As bass players, we often hold down things with repetitive lines that glue the groove together. These are often anchored to one position on the fretboard—a certain scale shape or "groove box," if you will—that frames the notes. In this lesson, we're going to examine these shapes and boxes and learn how to unlock their ability to spring forth a groove.

Major Scale Shapes

Let's start by looking at several major scale shapes in different positions. We'll work in the key of C for this lesson, but all this would apply to any key.

Shape 1

Let's play through the scale pattern in second position with the C root note on string 3. We'll call this Shape 1. Notice there are three additional notes available below the low root in this position.

Shape 2

Now let's move to fifth position and start with our pinky fretting C on string 4. We'll call this Shape 2. In this shape, we have two notes added below the root and one note added on top, above the octave root.

Shape 3

Now let's move to Shape 3, which has the root on string 4, fretted by the second finger. This is the same as Shape 1, only moved down a string set. We have one note added on the bottom and three added on top, above the root.

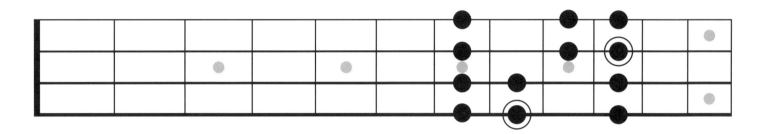

Shape 4

Now let's move to Shape 4. In this shape, we can't reach the high octave (which would be located a fret above the last note on string 1) without shifting out of position, but it contains a bunch of useful notes added on the bottom.

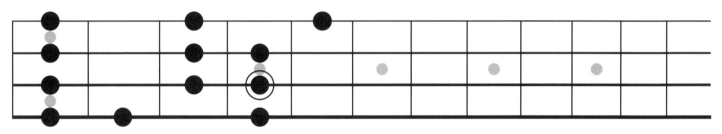

12fr

Shape 1 (Octave)

Moving up again brings us back to Shape 1 an octave higher.

12fr

Major Shapes: Boxing the Octaves and/or 5ths

Ok, now that we've gotten through twelve full frets on the fretboard, let's go back and place boxes around the shapes framed by the octaves or 5ths. Even though we played major scales for each position, these boxes will work for any major-type scale or mode, such as Mixolydian, as well.

Major Scale Box 1

Box 1 comes from Shape 1 and encompasses second position.

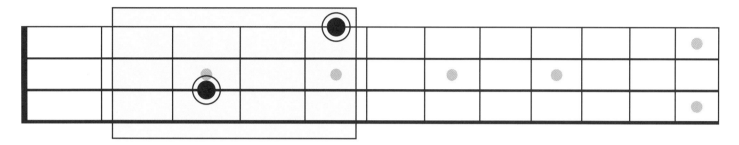

This is a great shape for grooving because you have a full octave of the scale along with a low 5th below the root, which you can exploit to come up with something like this.

Major Scale Box 2

Box 2 lies in fifth position.

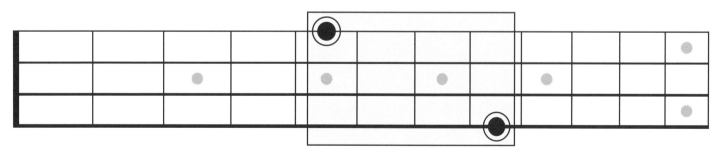

In this box, we have the low 6th—A in this case—which is a great, funky note. It works especially well when moving between a I and IV vamp, such as in this groove.

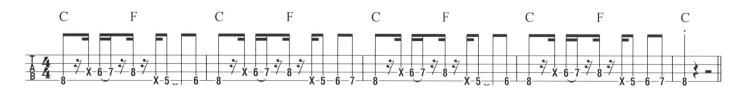

Box 3 puts us up in seventh position.

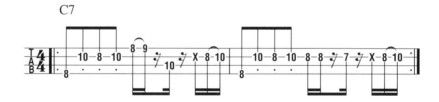

In this box, we have full access to the scale with several added notes on top. We can poke at those to get some funky things.

C7

Paul McCartney made use of this box for his line in "Lady Madonna." This is a nice example to demonstrate that it's common to temporarily stretch forward or backward to grab a note, as Paul does here with the C♮.

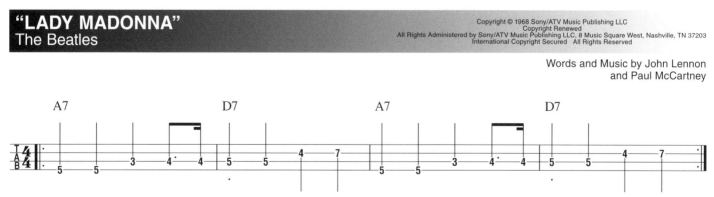

"LADY MADONNA"
The Beatles

Words and Music by John Lennon
and Paul McCartney

Major Scale Box 4

In Box 4, we don't have access to the octave, so our box is framed by the root and 5th. This puts us in twelfth position, so we're going to move it down an octave to open position.

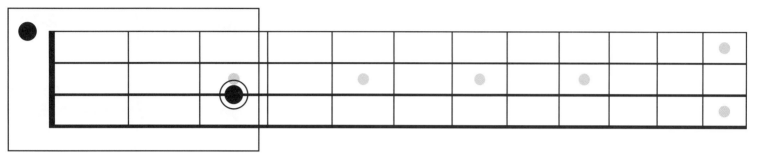

The cool thing about this box is the low 3rd—E in this case—on string 4. Check it out in this deep grooving line.

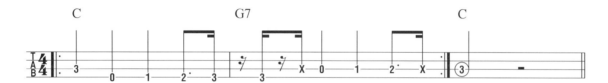

Bill Wyman grooves predominantly out of this box in the Rolling Stones's hit, "Beast of Burden." (Since it's in the key of E, he also throws in the open E at times as well.)

"BEAST OF BURDEN"
The Rolling Stones

Words and Music by Mick Jagger
and Keith Richards

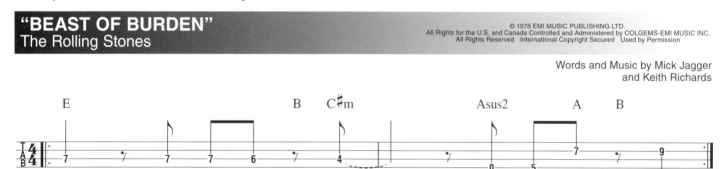

In the Marvin Gaye/Tammi Terrell duet, "Ain't Nothing Like the Real Thing," James Jamerson lays down a seriously funky line in E♭ from this box.

"AIN'T NOTHING LIKE THE REAL THING"
Marvin Gaye and Tammi Terrell

Words and Music by Nickolas Ashford
and Valerie Simpson

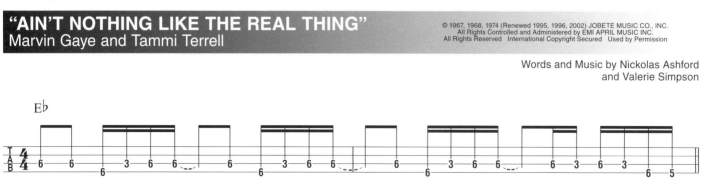

As we mentioned, Shape 5 would bring us an octave higher than we started.

Now let's take a look at all four boxes and see how they overlap on the fretboard.

Major Scale Boxes 1–4

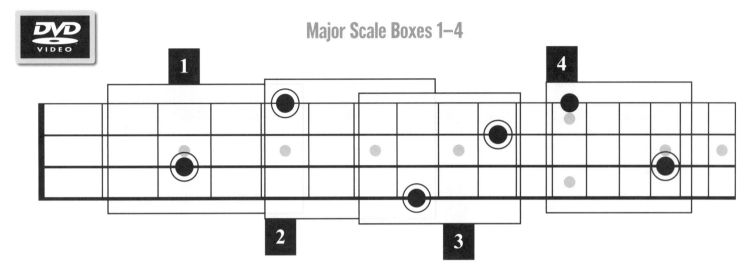

Notice that:

- Box 2 shares the high C note with Box 1.
- Box 3 shares the low C note with Box 2.
- And Box 4 would share the low C note with Box 1 if we were to continue again.

So you can see, all the frets are accounted for but one. This means you can comfortably cover nearly the entire fretboard from these four groove boxes.

Minor Scale Shapes

The boxes will be slightly modified when dealing with minor scales, so let's look at that. We'll play through the C minor scale in several positions the same way to generate the box shapes.

Shape 1

Our first shape will be in third position with our first finger fretting the C note on string 3. We have three added notes on the bottom of this one.

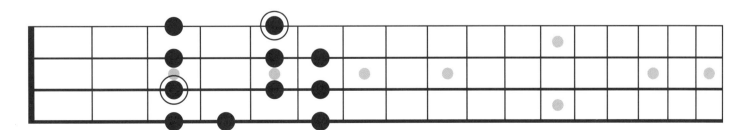

Shape 2

Shape 2 places our pinky on the low C note on string 4, which puts us in fifth position. This gives us two notes on top and only one on bottom when using the natural minor scale.

When we play out of the Dorian mode though, as we'll see in a bit, we'll also be able to access the 6th on bottom in this position, which is a great sound.

Shape 3

Shape 3 is the same as Shape 1 moved down a string set, so we have some added notes on top.

Shape 4

With Shape 4, we don't have access to a complete octave of the scale, but we do have many notes on bottom.

Moving up again would put us an octave up from Shape 1—the same as with the major shapes.

Again, though we played the natural minor scale to generate the boxes, we can use these with many minor-type scales or modes, including Dorian and Phrygian.

Minor Shapes: Boxing the Octaves and/or 5ths

Now let's generate the boxes around these shapes the same as we did with the major ones. Since we know the process now, let's just look at all four at once.

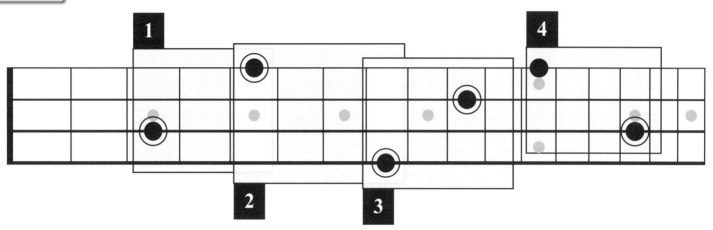

Notice:

- Box 2 shares the high C note from Box 1.
- Box 3 shares the low C note from Box 2.
- And Box 4 would share the low C note from Box 1 if we continued on.

Let's check out a few minor grooves from these boxes. Here's one from Box 1, which gives us the full octave scale with low G, A♭, and B♭ notes.

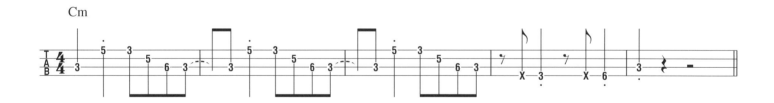

Roger Waters makes use of this box in B minor for his famous 7/4 pentatonic line in Pink Floyd's "Money."

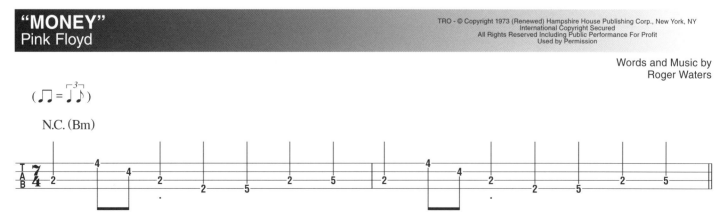

"MONEY"
Pink Floyd

Words and Music by
Roger Waters

Also in B minor, The Offspring's "Come Out and Play" features bassist Greg K. firmly rooted in the Box 1 position for the song's signature riff.

"COME OUT AND PLAY"
The Offspring

Words and Music by
Dexter Holland

And here's one from Box 2. This one's from the C Dorian mode, which is spelled C–D–E♭–F–G–A–B♭. Since the A note is on fret 5 of the fourth string, we can access it for a cool added tone on the bottom.

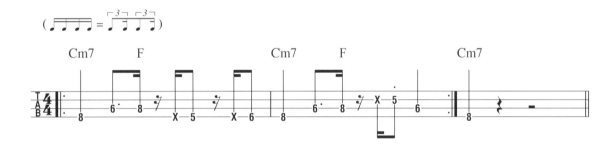

That low 6th sounds great down there, huh?

Box 4 is commonly used for minor pentatonic-based lines, as Lenny Kravitz demonstrates here with his funky E minor line in "Are You Gonna Go My Way."

"ARE YOU GONNA GO MY WAY"
Lenny Kravitz

Words by Lenny Kravitz
Music by Lenny Kravitz and Craig Ross

Here's Tommy Shannon's take on this box with his funky line in D from Stevie Ray Vaughan's "Couldn't Stand the Weather." Notice that he makes use of the full five-fret span from Shape 4 and also includes a few chromatic notes during the walk-up.

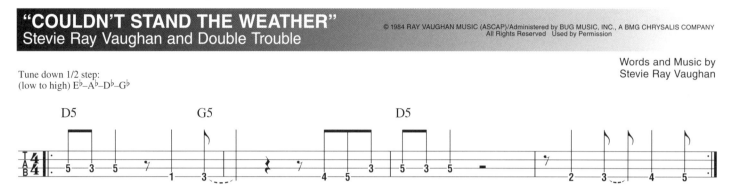

Well that wraps it up for this lesson. Hopefully, you've begun to see the potential that these groove boxes offer. They each have their own unique characteristics, so why not be familiar with them all and give yourself the option to choose the perfect one? Have fun and keep groovin'!

BASS BUILDERS

A series of technique book/CD packages created for the purposeful building and development of your chops. Each volume is written by an expert in that particular technique. And with the inclusion of audio, the added dimension of hearing exactly how to play particular grooves and techniques make these truly like private lessons.

BASS AEROBICS
by Jon Liebman
00696437 Book/CD Pack.....................$19.99

**BASS FITNESS –
AN EXERCISING HANDBOOK**
by Josquin des Prés
00660177.....................$10.99

BASS FOR BEGINNERS
by Glenn Letsch
00695099 Book/CD Pack.....................$19.95

BASS GROOVES
by Jon Liebman
00696028 Book/CD Pack.....................$19.99

BASS IMPROVISATION
by Ed Friedland
00695164 Book/CD Pack.....................$17.95

BLUES BASS
by Jon Liebman
00695235 Book/CD Pack.....................$19.95

BUILDING ROCK BASS LINES
by Ed Friedland
00695692 Book/CD Pack.....................$17.95

BUILDING WALKING BASS LINES
by Ed Friedland
00695008 Book/CD Pack.....................$19.99

**RON CARTER –
BUILDING JAZZ BASS LINES**
00841240 Book/CD Pack.....................$19.95

DICTIONARY OF BASS GROOVES
by Sean Malone
00695266 Book/CD Pack.....................$14.95

EXPANDING WALKING BASS LINES
by Ed Friedland
00695026 Book/CD Pack.....................$19.95

**FINGERBOARD HARMONY
FOR BASS**
by Gary Willis
00695043 Book/CD Pack.....................$17.95

FUNK BASS
by Jon Liebman
00699348 Book/CD Pack.....................$19.99

FUNK/FUSION BASS
by Jon Liebman
00696553 Book/CD Pack.....................$19.95

HIP-HOP BASS
by Josquin des Prés
00695589 Book/CD Pack.....................$14.95

JAZZ BASS
by Ed Friedland
00695084 Book/CD Pack.....................$17.95

**JERRY JEMMOTT –
BLUES AND RHYTHM &
BLUES BASS TECHNIQUE**
00695176 Book/CD Pack.....................$17.95

JUMP 'N' BLUES BASS
by Keith Rosier
00695292 Book/CD Pack.....................$16.95

**THE LOST ART OF
COUNTRY BASS**
by Keith Rosier
00695107 Book/CD Pack.....................$19.95

**PENTATONIC SCALES
FOR BASS**
by Ed Friedland
00696224 Book/CD Pack.....................$19.99

REGGAE BASS
by Ed Friedland
00695163 Book/CD Pack.....................$16.95

ROCK BASS
by Jon Liebman
00695083 Book/CD Pack.....................$17.95

'70S FUNK & DISCO BASS
by Josquin des Prés
00695614 Book/CD Pack.....................$15.99

**SIMPLIFIED SIGHT-READING
FOR BASS**
by Josquin des Prés
00695085 Book/CD Pack.....................$17.95

6-STRING BASSICS
by David Gross
00695221 Book/CD Pack.....................$12.95

SLAP BASS ESSENTIALS
by Josquin dés Pres and Bunny Brunel
00696563 Book/CD Pack.....................$19.95

**WORLD BEAT GROOVES
FOR BASS**
by Tony Cimorosi
00695335 Book/CD Pack.....................$14.95

HAL•LEONARD®
CORPORATION

7777 W. BLUEMOUND RD. P.O. BOX 13819 MILWAUKEE, WI 53213

Visit Hal Leonard Online at **www.halleonard.com**

HAL·LEONARD BASS PLAY·ALONG

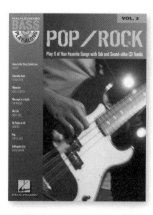

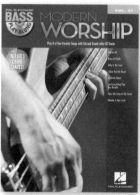

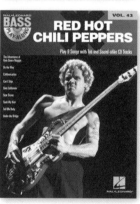

The Bass Play-Along™ Series will help you play your favorite songs quickly and easily! Just follow the tab, listen to the CD to hear how the bass should sound, and then play along using the separate backing tracks. The melody and lyrics are also included in the book in case you want to sing, or to simply help you follow along. The CD is enhanced so you can use your computer to adjust the recording to any tempo without changing pitch!

1. Rock
00699674 Book/CD Pack...................................$12.95

2. R&B
00699675 Book/CD Pack...................................$14.99

3. Pop/Rock
00699677 Book/CD Pack...................................$12.95

4. '90s Rock
00699679 Book/CD Pack...................................$12.95

5. Funk
00699680 Book/CD Pack...................................$12.95

6. Classic Rock
00699678 Book/CD Pack...................................$12.95

7. Hard Rock
00699676 Book/CD Pack...................................$14.95

8. Punk Rock
00699813 Book/CD Pack...................................$12.95

9. Blues
00699817 Book/CD Pack...................................$14.99

10. Jimi Hendrix Smash Hits
00699815 Book/CD Pack...................................$16.95

11. Country
00699818 Book/CD Pack...................................$12.95

12. Punk Classics
00699814 Book/CD Pack...................................$12.99

13. Lennon & McCartney
00699816 Book/CD Pack...................................$14.99

14. Modern Rock
00699821 Book/CD Pack...................................$14.99

15. Mainstream Rock
00699822 Book/CD Pack...................................$14.99

16. '80s Metal
00699825 Book/CD Pack...................................$16.99

17. Pop Metal
00699826 Book/CD Pack...................................$14.99

18. Blues Rock
00699828 Book/CD Pack...................................$14.99

19. Steely Dan
00700203 Book/CD Pack...................................$16.99

20. The Police
00700270 Book/CD Pack...................................$14.99

21. Rock Band – Modern Rock
00700705 Book/CD Pack...................................$14.95

22. Rock Band – Classic Rock
00700706 Book/CD Pack...................................$14.95

**23. Pink Floyd –
Dark Side of The Moon**
00700847 Book/CD Pack...................................$14.99

24. Weezer
00700960 Book/CD Pack...................................$14.99

25. Nirvana
00701047 Book/CD Pack...................................$14.99

26. Black Sabbath
00701180 Book/CD Pack...................................$16.99

27. Kiss
00701181 Book/CD Pack...................................$14.99

28. The Who
00701182 Book/CD Pack...................................$14.99

29. Eric Clapton
00701183 Book/CD Pack...................................$14.99

30. Early Rock
00701184 Book/CD Pack...................................$15.99

31. The 1970s
00701185 Book/CD Pack...................................$14.99

32. Disco
00701186 Book/CD Pack...................................$14.99

33. Christmas Hits
00701197 Book/CD Pack...................................$12.99

34. Easy Songs
00701480 Book/CD Pack...................................$12.99

35. Bob Marley
00701702 Book/CD Pack...................................$14.99

36. Aerosmith
00701886 Book/CD Pack...................................$14.99

37. Modern Worship
00701920 Book/CD Pack...................................$12.99

38. Avenged Sevenfold
00702386 Book/CD Pack...................................$16.99

40. AC/DC
14041594 Book/CD Pack...................................$16.99

41. U2
00702582 Book/CD Pack...................................$16.99

42. Red Hot Chili Peppers
00702991 Book/CD Pack...................................$19.99

45. Slipknot
00703201 Book/CD Pack...................................$16.99

FOR MORE INFORMATION, SEE YOUR LOCAL MUSIC DEALER,
OR WRITE TO:

HAL·LEONARD® CORPORATION
7777 W. BLUEMOUND RD. P.O. BOX 13819 MILWAUKEE, WI 53213

Visit Hal Leonard Online at **www.halleonard.com**
Prices, contents, and availability subject to change without notice.

0712